Other Books
by
Rory Miller

Violence: A Writer's Guide
Meditations on Violence
Facing Violence

Force Decisions

with Lawrence Kane

Scaling Force

DVDs

Facing Violence
Logic of Violence

Joint Locks

eBooks

Drills: Training for Sudden Violence
ChironTraining Volumes 1-6
Talking Them Through

Edited by Rory Miller

Campfire Tales from Hell

CHIRON
TRAINING
JOURNAL

WITH

RORY MILLER

For permission to reproduce part or all of this work,
contact Wyrd Goat Press, LLC
www.wyrdgoat.com

Concept by Rory A. Miller
Cover and interior book design by Kamila Z. Miller

ISBN-13: 978-0615968599
ISBN-10: 0615968597

Wyrd Goat Press First Edition, February 2014

TABLE OF CONTENTS

HOW TO USE THIS BOOK

My friend, this is mostly a blank book and you fill a blank book by writing and thinking. Especially thinking. And you're the author, that's why your name (or at least the blank line for it) comes first. I'm going to tell you how I intended for you to use it, but I'm not the boss of you. Do it your way.

I am going to insist on two things, though.

First of all, use the book. Write in it. There's nothing sadder than an unused blank book. You spent the money. The value in any thing is in its use.

Second, use it to make yourself better. Better at what? I don't care. Because of who I am, most likely you're a martial artist, LEO, Corrections Officer or soldier. So you can use the book to set goals and track progress to your certification or an Olympic medal or a flawless professional use of force. But if you want to track weightlifting or gardening or your mastery of a language or craft or just being nice to people, it's all good. Use the book to be better. You get to decide what better is.

Chiron is the Centaur who taught the ancient Greek warriors. He taught them to fight, to heal, to sing and to think. Protection and nurturing of life, art, and intelligence. All good stuff. Improve in any or all, but be better. That is your challenge and the only worthy quest of your life.

I'll have notes throughout, and I'll give you assignments (Yes. Homework. I'm a bastard.) I'll try to arrange it so that you write your thoughts before you see mine. If you are a beginner, fill the book before you read some of the stuff at the end, especially Building Blocks, Principles, and Concepts in Section 4. If you are already pretty competent, feel free to jump ahead. Just write down your thoughts before you read mine.

i

The Format of the Book

The very first section will be goal setting. What do you want to do? Who do you want to be? And what must you do to make that happen?

The second section is the training diary itself. The standard pages. The standard pages will have stuff for you to fill out.

It will start with <u>Date</u> and <u>Location</u>. Obvious. The next line will say <u>Instructor/Others</u>. Always cool to put the name of the teacher down. Even in informal training. If you picked up a life lesson from a homeless panhandler, give him a little credit. If you got an insight from a fellow student (or had a really challenging problem with a fellow student) that's notable. Note it.

<u>Activity</u>, simply, is what you did. As much or as little detail as you want.

<u>Impressions</u> is for stream-of-consciousness stuff. Don't overthink it or try to be literary or even accurate. If you think a technique is stupid, that's your impression. Write it down. If you are struggling with a throw it's okay to say, "I hate *tai otoshi*! I'll never get the timing!" Because five years from now, when it's your favorite throw, it's good for you and your students to remember it wasn't easy. As Musashi said, "It is difficult at first, but everything is difficult at first."

Impressions is also a good place for hunches and random thoughts you want to explore later: "Sensei doesn't do the footwork the way he tells us to. Why?" Following up on some of these questions will make an extraordinary difference in who you become and what you can do.

<u>Connections and Insights</u>. You're going to have a lot of 'aha' moments. This is where you put those. When you realize that "power transmitting through the *tan tien*" is really a mathematical metaphor for the center of gravity; or when you realize that two good instructors use

different words but are talking about the same thing, this is where it goes.

Don't ever let your insights inbreed. This section should not be only about your training. You should pick up insights about (and from) your daily life, your job, and unrelated training, like college classes or reading history. Almost everything in the world connects. The more of those connections you can see the more effective a person you can be.

<u>Goals</u>. What do you need to learn next? What do you want to do? What inspired you today? You can use this as a daily to-do list or work from "Connections and Insights" to plan your training or track your progress toward your lifetime goals.

This is important: You must become your own best teacher. A good teacher can trigger amazing growth. You must become that good teacher for yourself. No one knows your strengths, your weaknesses, your needs or your dreams like you do.

And revisit your goals occasionally, both the big ones from the first section and the little ones on each page. It's good to see your growth, and if you don't write it down, you'll be too close to see it.

<u>What did I learn today?</u> My mom used to say the day you stop learning is the day you start dying. Tom Brown, the Tracker, calls it the sacred question: "What is the lesson here?" Don't skip this section. If you learned something today, you are better than you were yesterday. And that's the whole point.

Section Three is for Instructor Profiles. Study your instructors the way they should be studying you. The better you understand a teacher, the better you can learn from that teacher.

<u>Name</u> is obvious.

<u>Discipline</u> is what the instructor is teaching. Usually the name of the class you signed up for.

<u>Dates Trained With</u> can be seminar dates or just write

in the day you started classes and the day you quit, if ever. I apologize if I am stating really obvious things but I have this image in my head of someone who goes to classes three nights a week for five years and tries to cram each individual date on the page.

<u>Contact Information</u> is for addresses and telephone numbers and e-mails and websites.

<u>Strengths</u>. And weaknesses, too. Every instructor is good at something (I hope) and none of us are perfect. In the Strengths section, jot down what a given instructor is really good at. Not just the techniques and skills. Nothing in this book is about the instructor, it is all about you. This is an exercise, for you, in observation. And it's not "Wendy is awesome at cross strangles so I'm going to pair up with her" So much as "Wendy is awesome at cross strangles. What makes her that way and how can I get that good?"

Don't limit it to technique. Some shitty fighters are excellent teachers. Write down how and why they are good at teaching. Some are excellent with kids, or dealing with emotional issues or just keeping the whole class comfortable.

Someday, this section will be a guide to the mentors that will help you be a great instructor. Provided you have the humility to never believe you are great and keep striving.

<u>Weaknesses</u>. The other side of the strength coin. There are some excellent instructors who suck at some things. Martial arts does some wear and tear and there are techniques I can teach that I'm too damaged to do. There are a few who don't get aspects of their own art and are too arrogant to admit it. There are some complete charlatans. Again, this is an observation exercise and an exercise in objectivity. Partially, this will create a list of what you don't want to be when you teach. And, sometimes, when you look at the list of weaknesses and strengths of your current instructors, you'll know it is time to move on.

<u>Personal Info</u> is for anything you think is relevant. Almost any person likes to be asked how their family is doing... it goes better if you know a family exists and have their names. Hobbies. Pets. The people sensei absolutely hates and will go on rants over. If you stumble across a hot button issue. Anything that makes it easier to understand or connect with the instructor.

<u>Notes</u> covers almost anything else.

<u>Questions</u>. A lot of these will come up in your regular training diary, but if you plan on attending a seminar or meet your instructor's instructor, start a profile for that person and include a list of questions you'd like to ask.

Section Four will go into Building Blocks, Principles, and Concepts. My examples will be heavily self-defense related, but I believe almost anything you desire to excel at can be broken down this way.

Building Blocks are the sets of basic skills you need to be competent.

Principles are the fundamentals that make other things work. The universals. For instance, good leverage makes everything better—striking, throwing or even stirring cake batter.

Concepts are the way skilled practitioners think. The things they understand that beginners and outsiders don't.

As you discover a principle or classify a building block, jot them down. I'll have a short list of mine in the back.

The very last blank section is for me. For us, if we ever meet. There is a list of my building blocks, principles, drills and lesson plans, each with a place to sign that you've studied them. A training record for the Chiron stuff.

Okay, boys and girls. You now have a book with a lot of blank pages. Get to work.

SECTION I
GOAL SETTING

M ost of this was taught to me by a gentleman named Steve Barnes. Steve gets immense credit for giving me the tools to stop drifting through life and start steering. I've been doing it for a while now and have bastardized it to suit my needs, so it will be rougher and less pure than what Steve does. You can contact him at www.diamondhour.com for his version and insights.

Planning has power. Executing plans has even more power, of course, but the plan comes first. Most people dither through their lives, waiting for opportunity, dodging problems, taking what comes. This is inherently passive. This is not a winning strategy. Do you like passive people? Admire them?

Quit being one.

So make a plan. What goes into the plan? Later. If you have a plan, steps to get to your goal, you have something to do. You have a quick test to see whether or not you are wasting time: Will this get me closer to the plan?

Musashi said, "Do nothing that is of no use." You want to be a black belt? Is watching a night of TV or going out drinking getting you closer to that? You want to strengthen your relationships? Spending hours alone at the gym might not be working for you.

Just having that benchmark, even if you only pay attention to it ten percent of the time, gives you a ten percent edge over almost everyone in the world. Because almost all of them are drifting, waiting for a perfect life to be handed to them.

I'll allow one 'what if' question on this part, and here it is:

What if I plan for a *good* job or a good mate and achieve the goal and miss out on the *perfect* one?

3

Sigh. I think that people have been handed their perfect lives twice in all of history. Both actors who were 'discovered' and one died under mysterious circumstances...

Less flippant, there are two things you already know. Working at 50 percent efficiency beats waiting at 100 percent. Going climbing with your second best friend beats waiting by the phone for your first best. And being a good, successful commercial artist beats hell out of being a posthumously discovered Old Master.

The second: it's not mutually exclusive. No one is going to give you your dream job if you can't be bothered to perform at your current job. The love interest of your dreams will never be attracted to you because you treat the people close to you poorly. Working for any goal draws attention, and it draws other opportunities and goals.

This 'what if' question is something the lazy part of your brain does to keep you on the couch, eating corn chips. Kill that voice in your head.

Steve advocates a three-goal model for living. You should set goals in all three areas and you should continuously work to improve your life in all three areas: Mind, body and spirit.

That might sound esoteric or vague, but Steve isn't a vague kind of guy. Success in all three can be easily measured. He has a set of yardsticks: If you are making a living wage at a job you love you are doing well mentally. If you are in good shape and good health, you are doing well physically. If you have healthy, enjoyable and friendly intimate relationships and close friends, you are doing well spiritually.

It is very simple. If you have a problem in any of these areas, the problem stems from you. If you balk at the choice of yardsticks ("Everybody hates me but I'm alright with God") you have a problem and are denying it.

Want to know who you are? You are damn close to the

average of your friends. If all your friends are assholes, I hate to be the one to tell you, but so are you. Possibly worse if you have no friends.

There are two general modes of planning. Most people work resources forward. They catalog what they have and decide what they can do with those resources. That's not the way we were taught to do it in emergency services.

In emergency services we were taught goals backward planning. Let's face it, if you are doing hostage rescue there is only one acceptable outcome.

So we would figure out the goal, figure out the steps necessary to achieve that goal and then gather the resources necessary to complete those steps.

That's what I want you to do. On the next page, I want you to start by writing where you want to be in X number of years. X isn't a typo. The first time I did this, at Steve's recommendation I shot for twenty years. Just by having a plan, I killed my twenty-year goals in about five years. Depending on age and how big your dreams are, it might make sense to set the goals for twenty years or for five.

Remember this is where you want to be physically (health and fitness); mentally (work and knowledge) and; spiritually (relationships, including the relationship with yourself). You may want to brainstorm it on scratch paper and enshrine the finished version here. That's the first page.

The second page of Goals, cut your time frame in half. If you wrote ten year goals, on the second page write down where you need to be in *five* years to be halfway there.

On the third page, cut it down by fifty percent again.

The rest of this you can do on scratch paper. What do you need to do this year to get to page three? This month? This week.

What are you going to do TODAY to bring your dream closer? Today's list and maybe this week's needs to be a note on your bathroom mirror. Do something today to bring your goals closer.

5

Notes

Long Term Goals

Long Term Goals- 50%

Long Term Goals 25%

SECTION II
TRAINING LOG

Date:

Location:

Instructors/Others:

Activity:

Impressions:

Connections and Insights:

Goals:

What did I learn new today?

The only defense against violent evil people is good
people who are more skilled at violence.

Date:

Location:

Instructors/Others:

Activity:

Impressions:

Connections and Insights:

Goals:

What did I learn new today?

To be sure about something you don't know is superstition.

Date:

Location:

Instructors/Others:

Activity:

Impressions:

Connections and Insights:

Goals:

What did I learn new today?

It is easier to instill confidence than competence.

Date:

Location:

Instructors/Others:

Activity:

Impressions:

Connections and Insights:

Goals:

What did I learn new today?

To manage fear you only need to believe you can do things.
To manage danger you must be able to do things.

Right now, shut your eyes and listen for five different sounds, feel for five different touches and (the hard one) try to identify five different smells

Date:

Location:

Instructors/Others:

Activity:

Impressions:

Connections and Insights:

Goals:

What did I learn new today?

Every last person can become amazing just by doing stuff. No one becomes amazing by sitting on their ass listening to other people's stories.

Date:

Location:

Instructors/Others:

Activity:

Impressions:

Connections and Insights:

Goals:

What did I learn new today?

You've spent your whole life learning to be a good person.
Don't forget you are also a perfectly good animal.

Date:

Location:

Instructors/Others:

Activity:

Impressions:

Connections and Insights:

Goals:

What did I learn new today?

You can take yourself seriously or the world seriously, just never both at the same time.

Date:

Location:

Instructors/Others:

Activity:

Impressions:

Connections and Insights:

Goals:

What did I learn new today?

"Good loser? I never want to lose enough to get good at it."- M. Phelps

Make a list of the things you should know (first aid, languages, economics, whatever).

Commit to knocking one off a year. Cross them off as you become proficient.

Date:

Location:

Instructors/Others:

Activity:

Impressions:

Connections and Insights:

Goals:

What did I learn new today?

Not everything can be de-escalated; not everyone can be talked down.

Date:

Location:

Instructors/Others:

Activity:

Impressions:

Connections and Insights:

Goals:

What did I learn new today?

Do not think dishonestly.- Musashi
Do not lie to yourself, ever.-RAM

Date:

Location:

Instructors/Others:

Activity:

Impressions:

Connections and Insights:

Goals:

What did I learn new today?

The Way is in training. -Musashi
*Work and learn hard, no one has ever improved
by sitting on their ass and waiting.*-RAM

24

Date:

Location:

Instructors/Others:

Activity:

Impressions:

Connections and Insights:

Goals:

What did I learn new today?

Become acquainted with every art. –Musashi
Never pass up an opportunity to learn how an artist or skilled craftsman thinks or sees the world. Seek out the best and listen.-RAM

Go to the library, pick out a book on a subject you know nothing about. Read it. You have one week.

Date:

Location:

Instructors/Others:

Activity:

Impressions:

Connections and Insights:

Goals:

What did I learn new today?

Know the ways of all professions. —Musashi
The world works because people do jobs. Learn about the
jobs that make the world work and how they interconnect.
Know ditch diggers and burger slingers, architects and
doctors and understand how they need each other.-RAM

Date:

Location:

Instructors/Others:

Activity:

Impressions:

Connections and Insights:

Goals:

What did I learn new today?

Distinguish between gain and loss in worldly matters. —Musashi
*Know what matters. Protect what is truly precious,
let go what is not. Do not lie to yourself about these
categories or let society lie to you.*-RAM

Date:

Location:

Instructors/Others:

Activity:

Impressions:

Connections and Insights:

Goals:

What did I learn new today?

Develop intuitive judgment and understanding for everything. -Musashi
*Trust your gut. Practice trusting your gut. Then practice
deciphering your gut so that you can explain it verbally and
you will develop intuition AND understanding.*-RAM

Date:

Location:

Instructors/Others:

Activity:

Impressions:

Connections and Insights:

Goals:

What did I learn new today?

> Perceive those things that cannot be seen. -Musashi
> *Everything leaves tracks. Everything affects other things.*
> *When you learn to read the tracks, you can deal with*
> *invisible problems, like past trauma in a student.*-RAM

Date:

Location:

Instructors/Others:

Activity:

Impressions:

Connections and Insights:

Goals:

What did I learn new today?

Pay attention to trivial things. -Musashi
*The tracks are in the small things, and small things
affect big things. The tightening around your eyes will
tell me more than a hundred of your words.*-RAM

31

If you had six months to live, what would you do? Make the list, then turn to page 46 (Not before)

Date:

Location:

Instructors/Others:

Activity:

Impressions:

Connections and Insights:

Goals:

What did I learn new today?

Do nothing that is of no use. -Musashi
My personal favorite- if you spend time doing something, it should make you or the world better. How many hours are wasted each day with TV shows that you won't remember next week or trivia or... how strong would you be if that time was spent working out? How much better could you make the world if the time was spent helping others?-RAM

Date:

Location:

Instructors/Others:

Activity:

Impressions:

Connections and Insights:

Goals:

What did I learn new today?

You do not get to pick what kind of bad things will happen to you.

Date:

Location:

Instructors/Others:

Activity:

Impressions:

Connections and Insights:

Goals:

What did I learn new today?

"I will still be here when the dust has cleared. Will you?" Tom McRae *Stronger than Dirt*

35

Find a studio that offers a free class in something you have no experience in. Take it. Don't let them know you have any experience at all. Brain like a sponge.

Date:

Location:

Instructors/Others:

Activity:

Impressions:

Connections and Insights:

Goals:

What did I learn new today?

As martial artists, you are studying the manufacture of cripples and corpses.

Date:

Location:

Instructors/Others:

Activity:

Impressions:

Connections and Insights:

Goals:

What did I learn new today?

"If Not Me, Then Who?"- Motto of Spetznaz counter-terrorism team Alpha.

Date:

Location:

Instructors/Others:

Activity:

Impressions:

Connections and Insights:

Goals:

What did I learn new today?

*"The nation that will insist upon drawing a broad line
of demarcation between the fighting man and the
thinking man is liable to find its fighting done by fools
and its thinking by cowards."* —Sir William Francis Butler

Date:

Location:

Instructors/Others:

Activity:

Impressions:

Connections and Insights:

Goals:

What did I learn new today?

"We sleep soundly in our beds because rough men stand ready
in the night to visit violence on those who would do us harm." -
Attributed both to George Orwell and to Winston Churchill

40

Predator day. Go to a public place—mall, festival, bar—I don't care. The more crowded the better.

1) Spend some time noticing who you would pick to victimize if you were a bad guy and who you would leave alone. Let your gut make the decision first, then figure out the clues with your brains later.

2) Pick someone at random. See how long you can stay within five feet of him or her without being noticed.

3) Pick someone at random. Make that person bump into you, entirely their fault.

4) Story telling. Pick someone and tell a story about who he or she is. Don't try to be accurate or deductive. Let the story come into your mind and then study the person for the corroborative details. Your subconscious is better at this than your conscious.

5) Ask a stranger for directions or a cigarette, the standard crook 'interview' questions.

Date:

Location:

Instructors/Others:

Activity:

Impressions:

Connections and Insights:

Goals:

What did I learn new today?

Inveniam viam aut faciam - my team's motto:
"We will find a way or we will make one."

Date:

Location:

Instructors/Others:

Activity:

Impressions:

Connections and Insights:

Goals:

What did I learn new today?

"This is the true joy in life - being used for a purpose recognized by yourself as a mighty one; being thoroughly worn out before you are thrown on the scrap heap; being a force of nature instead of a feverish selfish little clod of ailments and grievances complaining that the world will not devote itself to making you happy." - George Bernard Shaw

Date:

Location:

Instructors/Others:

Activity:

Impressions:

Connections and Insights:

Goals:

What did I learn new today?

Trust is the greatest reward for the fighting man-
Niccolo Machiavelli, "On War" (from memory).

Date:

Location:

Instructors/Others:

Activity:

Impressions:

Connections and Insights:

Goals:

What did I learn new today?

Men don't follow orders, they follow men.

Date:

Location:

Instructors/Others:

Activity:

Impressions:

Connections and Insights:

Goals:

What did I learn new today?

Look at your list. Are you doing that now? Why not? Get to work.

Date:

Location:

Instructors/Others:

Activity:

Impressions:

Connections and Insights:

Goals:

What did I learn new today?

"The right thing to do is rarely the easy thing to do."-?

Date:

Location:

Instructors/Others:

Activity:

Impressions:

Connections and Insights:

Goals:

What did I learn new today?

"We few, we happy few, we band of brothers; For he today that sheds his blood with me shall be my brother"- William Shakespeare "*Henry V*"

Date:

Location:

Instructors/Others:

Activity:

Impressions:

Connections and Insights:

Goals:

What did I learn new today?

"Bones heal, chicks dig scars, pain is temporary." - Evel Knievel

Date:

Location:

Instructors/Others:

Activity:

Impressions:

Connections and Insights:

Goals:

What did I learn new today?

"The unforgivable crime is soft hitting. Do not hit at all if it can
be avoided; but never hit softly." Theodore Roosevelt

You have been chosen to teach one class to the top practitioners in the world. What's the lesson plan?

Date:

Location:

Instructors/Others:

Activity:

Impressions:

Connections and Insights:

Goals:

What did I learn new today?

*"No matter whether a person belongs to the upper ranks
or the lower, if he has not put his life on the line at least
once he has cause for shame."* -Nabeshima Naoshige

Date:

Location:

Instructors/Others:

Activity:

Impressions:

Connections and Insights:

Goals:

What did I learn new today?

"The foundation of a man's duty as a man is in truth. Beyond this there is nothing to be said." --Torii Mototada

Date:

Location:

Instructors/Others:

Activity:

Impressions:

Connections and Insights:

Goals:

What did I learn new today?

"To laugh often and love much; to win the respect of intelligent persons and the affection of children; to earn the approbation of honest citizens and endure the betrayal of false friends; to appreciate beauty; to find the best in others; to give of one's self; to leave the world a bit better, whether by a healthy child, a garden patch or a redeemed social condition; to have played and laughed with enthusiasm and sung with exultation; to know even one life has breathed easier because you have lived - this is to have succeeded."—Ralph Waldo Emerson

Date:

Location:

Instructors/Others:

Activity:

Impressions:

Connections and Insights:

Goals:

What did I learn new today?

"The bitch about ignorance isn't what you don't know. It's
what you think you know that isn't so."--?

Start a conversation with a stranger. Find out what they do for a living, where they live (not necessarily exact address) and one personal fact. While NOT giving the same information about yourself.

Date:

Location:

Instructors/Others:

Activity:

Impressions:

Connections and Insights:

Goals:

What did I learn new today?

Newton is my shihan

Date:

Location:

Instructors/Others:

Activity:

Impressions:

Connections and Insights:

Goals:

What did I learn new today?

"Kata should be practiced in an air of distrust." Shuzuk Shiitama

Date:

Location:

Instructors/Others:

Activity:

Impressions:

Connections and Insights:

Goals:

What did I learn new today?

Date:

Location:

Instructors/Others:

Activity:

Impressions:

Connections and Insights:

Goals:

What did I learn new today?

Our fears and dreads mark the edges of our comfort zones. Doing the things we hate and fear to do is exactly what we need for maximum growth. And it's not always physical fear, far more often it is the imaginary fear of embarrassment.

You must distinguish between fear and danger. Some things you don't challenge. You may have a morbid fear of being eaten alive by dogs, it is not learning to control your fear to be eaten alive.

It might be skydiving, it might be singing in public. On this page, make a list of your fears. At least ten of them. And then face them.

Date:

Location:

Instructors/Others:

Activity:

Impressions:

Connections and Insights:

Goals:

What did I learn new today?

Date:

Location:

Instructors/Others:

Activity:

Impressions:

Connections and Insights:

Goals:

What did I learn new today?

Date:

Location:

Instructors/Others:

Activity:

Impressions:

Connections and Insights:

Goals:

What did I learn new today?

Quit looking for the right woman (or man). Work to become
the worthy when she (or he) shows up.

Date:

Location:

Instructors/Others:

Activity:

Impressions:

Connections and Insights:

Goals:

What did I learn new today?

"Train Hard. Be Humble. Fight Dirty." Motto of Portland Jujitsu.

You are being attacked from your rear flank right now. What improvised weapons are at hand?

Date:

Location:

Instructors/Others:

Activity:

Impressions:

Connections and Insights:

Goals:

What did I learn new today?

To believe that there is always a reasonable solution is, itself, unreasonable.
When his definition of a win includes seeing you broken
and begging, there is no win-win solution.

Date:

Location:

Instructors/Others:

Activity:

Impressions:

Connections and Insights:

Goals:

What did I learn new today?

"Life is pain, Highness. Anyone who says differently is selling something."- Wesley, *The Princess Bride*

Date:

Location:

Instructors/Others:

Activity:

Impressions:

Connections and Insights:

Goals:

What did I learn new today?

There is evil in the world. But there is a lot more stupidity, laziness and selfishness.

Date:

Location:

Instructors/Others:

Activity:

Impressions:

Connections and Insights:

Goals:

What did I learn new today?

Life is easy. I see stupid people do it all the time.

Every system or style, not just of martial arts, but almost everything, arose in a certain time and place. It dealt, successfully, with a specific problem, in a specific context, with a specific technology and even social assumptions.

Can you figure out the assumptions of your primary style? Write them down.

Date:

Location:

Instructors/Others:

Activity:

Impressions:

Connections and Insights:

Goals:

What did I learn new today?

Interpersonal violence is a complex problem that requires simple solutions.

Date:

Location:

Instructors/Others:

Activity:

Impressions:

Connections and Insights:

Goals:

What did I learn new today?

If an art takes thirty years to master and claims to have arisen when the life expectancy was thirty-four, you should be sceptical about other parts, too.

Date:

Location:

Instructors/Others:

Activity:

Impressions:

Connections and Insights:

Goals:

What did I learn new today?

You don't have to get hit in the face to know it hurts. You do have
to get hit in the face to know if you can deal with it.

Date:

Location:

Instructors/Others:

Activity:

Impressions:

Connections and Insights:

Goals:

What did I learn new today?

Pain, fear and chaos are the natural elements of a fight.
They have to be part of any true training.

Choose two places where you spend time, e.g. home and work. Catalog: all exits; locations of fire extinguishers; surveillance cameras, if any; first aid kits and AEDs; electric, water and gas shut-offs.

Date:

Location:

Instructors/Others:

Activity:

Impressions:

Connections and Insights:

Goals:

What did I learn new today?

The natural progression for self-defense instruction is to, first, make an emotionally safe place to do physically dangerous things. Then, when the student is ready, make a physically safe place to do emotionally dangerous things.

Date:

Location:

Instructors/Others:

Activity:

Impressions:

Connections and Insights:

Goals:

What did I learn new today?

"We do not treat criminals like ladies and gentlemen because they are.
We treat them like ladies and gentlemen because *we* are."
--? From memory. In Jack Hoban's Ethical Protector class.

Date:

Location:

Instructors/Others:

Activity:

Impressions:

Connections and Insights:

Goals:

What did I learn new today?

The many paths lead to the top of very different mountains.

Through some mystical means, you know that a certain kid will become the ultimate (martial atist, warrior, whatever) of the next generation...and you get to teach his very first ever class. What's the lesson plan?

Date:

Location:

Instructors/Others:

Activity:

Impressions:

Connections and Insights:

Goals:

What did I learn new today?

Enlightenment is not the presence of knowledge, it's the absence
of bullshit. Or illusion, in the traditional parlance.

Date:

Location:

Instructors/Others:

Activity:

Impressions:

Connections and Insights:

Goals:

What did I learn new today?

You are made of meat. The Tiger has not forgotten that.

Date:

Location:

Instructors/Others:

Activity:

Impressions:

Connections and Insights:

Goals:

What did I learn new today?

Date:

Location:

Instructors/Others:

Activity:

Impressions:

Connections and Insights:

Goals:

What did I learn new today?

"Fear" "Anger" and "Infatuation" are just labels for adrenaline.
You can use the adrenaline if you don't name it.

If you could go back in time and tell yourself one thing, what would it be? And at what age? Have you told your children or students this thing?

Date:

Location:

Instructors/Others:

Activity:

Impressions:

Connections and Insights:

Goals:

What did I learn new today?

"In...all the things that we call 'noble' dogs are lightyears ahead of the jumped-up apes who own them."—R.A. Ellis "Horrible Stories I Told my Children"

Date:

Location:

Instructors/Others:

Activity:

Impressions:

Connections and Insights:

Goals:

What did I learn new today?

"Communication without intelligence is noise; Intelligence without communication is irrelevant." --Gen. Alfred. M. Gray, USMC

87

What is your greatest weakness? Strength? Vulnerability? How would a bad guy get to you?

Date:

Location:

Instructors/Others:

Activity:

Impressions:

Connections and Insights:

Goals:

What did I learn new today?

The seven natural strategies: Freeze (or hide) Flight, Fight,
Posture, Submit, Hunt, and Gather Intel.

Date:

Location:

Instructors/Others:

Activity:

Impressions:

Connections and Insights:

Goals:

What did I learn new today?

Date:

Location:

Instructors/Others:

Activity:

Impressions:

Connections and Insights:

Goals:

What did I learn new today?

We tend to judge other people by their actions but ourselves
by our intentions. (Paraphrased from Steven Covey)
Only actions count-RAM

Date:

Location:

Instructors/Others:

Activity:

Impressions:

Connections and Insights:

Goals:

What did I learn new today?

Joint injuries are like predators. They'll just come back when you're older and weaker.

Date:

Location:

Instructors/Others:

Activity:

Impressions:

Connections and Insights:

Goals:

What did I learn new today?

To fighters, time isn't a medium that you move in. It is a
resource that can be saved, wasted, spent-- or stolen.

Date:

Location:

Instructors/Others:

Activity:

Impressions:

Connections and Insights:

Goals:

What did I learn new today?

If you don't hate your workout routine a little, it's time to up the intensity.

An epistemology is how a society or individual determines that something is true. Most of the things that we believe have little or no basis in personal experience. Only people who spend time at sea, or who have an understanding of applied geometry and optics and have seen a lunar eclipse have any direct experience that the earth is round. To have a legitimate personal opinion on whether Fords or Chevys are better, you would have to run at least ten cars of each type until they failed. Most of what we 'know' we don't actually know, but we believe it to be true.

For a page, I want you to explore your personal epistemology. The things you heard before a certain age from your parents? What your friends insist is true? This news source is good but that news source is clearly biased?

What is your personal epistemology?

Date:

Location:

Instructors/Others:

Activity:

Impressions:

Connections and Insights:

Goals:

What did I learn new today?

There is only one way to stop getting older.

Date:

Location:

Instructors/Others:

Activity:

Impressions:

Connections and Insights:

Goals:

What did I learn new today?

You can't be certified by someone else in your ability to think for yourself.

Date:

Location:

Instructors/Others:

Activity:

Impressions:

Connections and Insights:

Goals:

What did I learn new today?

Everything in your training should make you stronger, smarter and more independent.

Date:

Location:

Instructors/Others:

Activity:

Impressions:

Connections and Insights:

Goals:

What did I learn new today?

You can't teach someone to stand up while demanding that they bow.

Date:

Location:

Instructors/Others:

Activity:

Impressions:

Connections and Insights:

Goals:

What did I learn new today?

Your job as a student is to become better than your instructor. Your job as an instructor is to make your students better than you. Anything less is disrespectful.

Date:

Location:

Instructors/Others:

Activity:

Impressions:

Connections and Insights:

Goals:

What did I learn new today?

The problems are mental. If you can't be rude to a
stranger, what are the odds you can hit one?

Date:

Location:

Instructors/Others:

Activity:

Impressions:

Connections and Insights:

Goals:

What did I learn new today?

The dream is damned and dreamer too, if dreaming's all that dreamers do.

Pick one of your Principles (see page 150) and design an exercise to teach it.

THE LAST PIECE OF ADVICE

Most of you will never be attacked. Spending 2000 hours over ten years to save 48 hours in a hospital doesn't make mathematical sense. Spending $4000 over ten years to save the $100 in your wallet from a mugger doesn't make mathematical sense. And defining your life by your fears doesn't make sense on any level.

Never train out of fear. Train because you love training.

SECTION III
INSTRUCTOR PROFILES

INSTRUCTOR

Name:

Discipline:

Dates trained with:

Contact Information:

Strengths:

Weaknesses:

Personal Information:

Notes:

Questions:

INSTRUCTOR

Name:

Discipline:

Dates trained with:

Contact Information:

Strengths:

Weaknesses:

Personal Information:

Notes:

Questions:

INSTRUCTOR

Name:

Discipline:

Dates trained with:

Contact Information:

Strengths:

Weaknesses:

Personal Information:

Notes:

Questions:

INSTRUCTOR

Name:

Discipline:

Dates trained with:

Contact Information:

Strengths:

Weaknesses:

Personal Information:

Notes:

Questions:

INSTRUCTOR

Name:

Discipline:

Dates trained with:

Contact Information:

Strengths:

Weaknesses:

Personal Information:

Notes:

Questions:

INSTRUCTOR

Name:

Discipline:

Dates trained with:

Contact Information:

Strengths:

Weaknesses:

Personal Information:

Notes:

Questions:

INSTRUCTOR

Name:

Discipline:

Dates trained with:

Contact Information:

Strengths:

Weaknesses:

Personal Information:

Notes:

Questions:

INSTRUCTOR

Name:

Discipline:

Dates trained with:

Contact Information:

Strengths:

Weaknesses:

Personal Information:

Notes:

Questions:

INSTRUCTOR

Name:

Discipline:

Dates trained with:

Contact Information:

Strengths:

Weaknesses:

Personal Information:

Notes:

Questions:

INSTRUCTOR

Name:

Discipline:

Dates trained with:

Contact Information:

Strengths:

Weaknesses:

Personal Information:

Notes:

Questions:

SECTION IV
BUILDING BLOCKS, PRINCIPLES & CONCEPTS

Building Blocks are the basic classes of techniques. They are also the 'sweet spot' for codifying useful information. Humans can look at the same things in big, sweeping generalities (impact!) or in tiny detail (middle-knuckle extended horizontal fist.) Too much detail and you have fighters trying to fight from memory, using the wrong part of their brains. Too general, and it is almost impossible to teach and therefore impossible to learn. "Become one with your opponent" is both a complete fighting philosophy and completely useless.

So this section is just a list of your building blocks, broken down the way that makes sense to you. You might have 'Hand strikes. Knee strikes. Kicks. Elbows. Head butts.' For five things. Or cover the exact same material with 'Power generation. Targets. Weapon conformation."

And if you decided this book is about gardening instead of beating people up your building blocks might include soil amelioration and pruning.

There will be two pages for this. It's just a list. If you need more than two pages you are probably, in my opinion, breaking things down too far. But I could be wrong.

After the section, there will be my list of building blocks. If you are experienced, I strongly encourage you to write your list before looking at mine. The synergy is strongest if people do their best separately first.

Principles are the things that make other things work. When you discover something common to all systems, grappling, striking, throwing or weapons, you have a principle. One example is leverage. Good leverage makes things better. Poor leverage makes things worse. I've only identified a handful of really universal principles and some of them are lumps of ideas. You'll get it when you see my list. After you write yours, please.

And your list will change over time. That's called learning and that's good. If we ever meet to initial the fifth section of the book, I'm going through the whole book and if it's getting full there should be some things crossed out. Fair warning.

Four Pages for this.

Concepts are the ways of thinking. If you are good at anything—driving, writing, fighting, anything—you do not think about that subject the way a beginner thinks. A blackbelt doesn't look at questions the same as a beginner...and someone who has had a hundred fights doesn't look at them like a blackbelt.

Changes in thinking are almost invisible. Once you learn to see or think in a new way, you will think that you have always known it. You will notice your changes by listening to beginners. An example, from my blog:

Devin is an excellent technical fighter who is searching for the answer, the one right way. He is young and believes that there is a right answer and a best choice in all situations. A lot was said last night about how old fighters look at things like attitude versus skill; justice versus duty; right versus effective; the cost even of the best choice in some situations; what it means and what it doesn't -- much more than most non-professionals have ever heard.

He asked at one point about what allowed us to go solo into a cell with someone in obvious excited delirium and talk them down. He asked if we just always convinced ourselves that we would win.

Sean and I both said, after a lot of thought, that we hadn't thought in terms of winning in years. We couldn't even put our finger on when or why that had become an irrelevant concept- but Sean pointed out that it was probably because we don't think of it as a contest.

Concepts will be big and will change much. It will change more the deeper you go. And changing your way of thinking can meet a lot of internal resistance. Embrace the growth. Ten pages.

MY BUILDING BLOCKS

RORY'S BUILDING BLOCKS

◊ Ukemi (break falls, how to land safely)

◊ Irimi (Entries, how to safely close on a threat)

◊ Takedowns

◊ Locks

◊ Power Generation

◊ Hand strikes

◊ Foot strikes

◊ Infighting Strikes

◊ Infighting kicks

◊ Targets

◊ Crashing (Bodyweight smashes into people)

◊ Manhandling (How to move a body and exploit the effort when someone tries to move you)

◊ Leverage Points (The places on the body that have the biggest payoff in terms of leverage)

◊ Counter assault (Operant conditioned responses to ambushes and suckerpunches)

◊ Ground Movement (Basic Grappling)

◊ Ground Controls (Pins and positioning and escapes)

◊ Striking from the ground

◊ Pain

◊ Core Defense (using elbows and shoulders as primary defensive tools)

◊ Puppet Mastering (The infighting version of Manhandling, using your grip to manipulate the threat through his core, e.g. making him abort a kick or miss a punch by pushing or pulling his shoulder)

◊ Shime waza and neck breaks

◊ Weapon Retention (Mostly for cops)

◊ Spine Controls

◊ Integration (A training system to forge all of the Building Blocks into a single fighting system)

MY PRINCIPLES

RORY'S LIST OF PRINCIPLES

◊ Leverage: the longer the lever arm, the more power you can apply. In a wristlock, the diagonal across the back of the hand is the longest lever arm; in a sweep, the higher the force on the body and lower the force on the leg, the harder the throw is to resist...

◊ Structure: Using bone instead of muscle. Bone doesn't get tired. Unstructured joints create shock absorbers that bleed power off into space when you strike. The body is connected so if you work it right, a grip on the threat's shoulder (or, sometimes, locked wrist) can control his feet. Defensively, good structure forces the threat, especially grapplers, to work against bone. They can bend joints and exhaust muscle, but they can't compress bone.

◊ Balance: Your contact points with the ground make a base. Your Center of gravity (CoG) stays over that base. If the CoG leaves the base, you lose balance; if the base can't get back under the CoG, you fall or roll. That simple. Control yours, manipulate the threat's. And two people in a clinch can be seen as two bases and CoGs-- or as a four-legged creature with a shared CoG, which you can control.

◊ 2-Way action: When possible, hit things from two directions: push _and_ pull locks; crash _and_ sweep takedowns; exercise _and_ eat right to get fit.

◊ Gravity: Gravity doesn't telegraph, it is stronger than you and you can't accelerate at 32 ft/sec^2. Whenever possible, use your weight instead of or in addition to your strength.

◊ Action/Reaction: He who moves first lands first.

Take and keep the initiative.

◊ Gifts: Each of the Threat's attacks comes with momentum you can exploit. The world is full of obstacles and weapons you can use. Learn to see.

◊ Space and Time: A big one and complex. This includes ranges, fighting against emptiness instead of force, creating and using deadzones to be safe in a fight, controlling pace, mentally altering your opponent's perception of time and distance, creating freezes, feinting... this one is big.

◊ Line and Circle: The geometry of conflict. Linear and circular movements have different possibilities, power generations, strengths and weaknesses.

◊ Environment: Use everything around you, from terrain to the social attitudes of the audience. This has strategic, tactical and immediate applications.

◊ Targeting: Some places hurt more than others. Hit the one that hurts most.

MY CONCEPTS

RORY'S LIST OF CONCEPTS

◊ Sparring is not dueling is not fighting is not combat is not Defensive Tactics is not self-defense: The skills, mindsets and circumstances are different. Being really good at one aspect doesn't imply you can handle yourself in another situation. Know what you are training for and what you are not training for.

◊ Violence Dynamics: If you don't understand how bad guys think, act, and attack, your training is a crapshoot. Some effective techniques for certain kinds of violence will backfire against other kinds.

◊ 4/5 Split. 4/5 refers to a specific level in our force continuum. To put it in civilian terms, you are either fighting for control (4-) or fighting for your life (5+). The mindsets, skills, attitudes and techniques between these levels are completely unrelated. If you use level 5 techniques in a level 4 situation, you will be sued. If you attempt to use level 4 in a level 5 situation, you will be hurt or killed.

◊ Point of No Return. Once bad things kick off, it is on until you can make yourself safe. No exceptions.

◊ SSR. The Survival Stress Response. Adrenaline. It affects everything.

◊ 4 Factors. Every force encounter involves four factors: you, the threat or threats, the environment, and luck. The better you know each factor and the interplay between the factors, the more you can do.

◊ 3 Stages. If an assault goes physical, you have to have three sets of skills for the stages. Operant conditioned counter-assault to get past the first quarter second of the ambush; the ability to break out of the freeze that an ambush nearly always induces; and then the skills to fight.

◊ Teaching, Training, Conditioning and Play. There are four ways stuff gets into your student's heads. If you want them to use it under stress, concentrate on conditioning and play. If you want them to be good teachers and researchers, concentrate on Teaching (words). If you want them to be easily controlled robots, concentrate on rote drills (training).

◊ OODA. Understand how decisions are made and how to manipulate the process. Observe, Orient, Decide, Act. Accelerate your steps and try to spike the opponent's process.

◊ Training Flaws. Unless you regularly send people to the hospital or the morgue in training, your training has deliberate safety protocols built in that *will* bite you on the ass if you ever need to send someone to the hospital or the morgue. The harder and faster you train, the harder the safety flaws ingrain. Know what your flaws are and use other training methods to counter them.

◊ Adrenaline and Truth. Anything you experience under an adrenaline load feels more real. It doesn't make it more real. Be very, very cautious not to confuse intensity with truth.

◊ Effects and Actions. Mostly for training, there are really only a few things you can do to a human body—you can move the person or part of the person, cause pain, cause damage or cause shock. Unarmed, there are only a few ways to get those effects: Striking, gouging, locking, take downs, strangulation and biting. This fighting stuff isn't that complicated.

◊ Jeff's Rules. From Deputy US Marshal Jeff Jones. Everything you teach must: 1) Have a tactical use, 2) Work whether you are moving or standing still, 3) Work under the SSR and, 4) Work whether you can see or not.

◊ Reframing. Sometimes you can change the problem instead of trying to solve the problem. If someone wants to fight you, solving the problem is figuring out how to win the fight. Reframing is changing the desire to have the fight in the first place.

◊ Ju. Dave Sumner, my Sosuishitsu jujutsu sensei defined 'ju' as "Tactical adaptability." No better way to say it. The essence of survival is your ability to adapt.

◊ Fight to the goal. It should never go to force unless there is a specific goal (say, to escape or to handcuff.) Every last thing, from strategy to technique, must serve that goal. It may not be the goal you've spent decades training for. Tough. Adapt.

◊ Fight the Mind. Except at the very far end of dealing with animals or extremely emotionally disturbed persons, you are not fighting a body but a mind. Your goal is to break the will. Even when the goal is physical or the person's will won't break, you can still use the mind to affect the body. Surprise, pain, sound, and positioning are just a few ways.

◊ Acting. Acting is refined physical communication. So is fighting. In training you want to play a realistic bad guy when appropriate. In an actual or potential force situation the persona you present will direct how the bad guy will approach and react.

◊ Discretionary Time. From Gordon Graham. Understand when you have time and when you don't. If you're under threat, you <u>aren't</u> under attack—so plan, communicate and gather resources. If you are under attack, it is too late to plan. Fight or run.

◊ Golden Rule of Combat. "Your most powerful weapon applied to your opponent's greatest vulnerability at his time of maximum imbalance."

◊ Golden Move. Every single motion in a fight should accomplish four things: Protect you, damage the threat, improve your position and worsen the threat's position. That's the gold standard.

◊ Fight Emptiness. We are wired to oppose force with force. Knock that shit off. Slip sideways to the pin or push. Step out of the lock through the big gaping hole. Get behind the threat instead of staying on the X.

◊ Multi-Layer. All Force incidents happen in a relationship and on a terrain. They involve physicality, but also emotions and social conditioning. They have an element of communication. Manipulate as many of these simultaneously as you can. Knocking someone down while saying, "Please, don't make me hurt you," affects the threat and witnesses very differently than knocking the same threat down with, "I swear to God I'm going to fucking kill you!"

◊ Complacency Kills. You will never be good enough. There is no such thing as a 'Survival level of skill.' There is stuff out there that will crush you like a bug on a windshield no matter who you are. All force incidents are dangerous and there are no guarantees. Bring your 'A' game. Don't even have a 'B' game.

◊ There is no Sure. There are no experts in this subject, nothing that guarantees a good outcome. If you ever feel sure about anything, just assume you're wrong.

SECTION V
CHIRON
TRAINING

These are the things I think are important and teach regularly. If you have an instructor you trust to test your competency, it's cool to have him or her sign off. Or me.

Building Blocks

◊   Ukemi

◊   Irimi

◊   Takedowns

◊   Locks

◊   Power Generation

◊   Hand strikes

◊   Foot strikes

◊   Infighting Strikes

◊   Infighting kicks

◊   Targets

◊   Crashing

◊   Manhandling

Principles

◊   Leverage

◊   Structure

◊   Balance

◊   2-Way action

◊   Gravity

◊   Action/Reaction

◊   Gifts

◊   Space and Time

◊   Line and Circle

◊   Environment

◊   Targeting

<u>DRILLS:</u> The designators refer to the full descriptions found in the manual *Drills: Training for Sudden Violence*

◊   OS1: The One-Step

◊   OS2: Four Option One-Step

◊   OS3: The Baby Drill

◊   OS4: Slow Man Drills

◊   OS5: Three-Way Coaching

◊   OS6: Dance Floor Melee

◊   OS7: Frisk Fighting

◊   OS8: Environmental Fighting

◊   OS9: The Brawl

◊   B1: Blindfolded Defense

◊   B2: Blindfolded Targeting

◊   B3: Core Fighting

Formal Presentations

◊   Introduction to Violence (Ambushes and Thugs)

Day #1

◊   Introduction to Violence (Ambushes and Thugs)

Day #2

◊   Logic of Violence

◊   Logic of Violence and Principles

◊   Conflict Communications Basic

◊   Conflict Communications Specialty Modules

◊   Threat Assessment

◊   Scenario Training

◊   Infighting

◊   Chiron Defensive Tactics

ABOUT THE AUTHOR
So, who are you? Be honest.

A Friend of Memory

Addresses & Observations

Wyrd Goat Books has a selection of unique blank books to catalogue and organize your most important information, including the dossier address books *A Friend of Memory* and *An Intimate Friend of Memory*

http://wyrdgoat.com

Made in the USA
Columbia, SC
15 August 2017